Cover illustration
The Chinese flagship Yangwu and the armed transport Fupo under attack by French torpedo boats No. 46 and No. 45. Combat naval de Fou-Tchéou ('The naval battle at Foochow'), by Charles Kuwasseg, 1885

THE
FRENCH AT FOOCHOW,

BY

JAMES F. ROCHE,
L. L. COWEN, } U. S. NAVY.

The Naval & Military Press Ltd

Published by

The Naval & Military Press Ltd
Unit 5 Riverside, Brambleside
Bellbrook Industrial Estate
Uckfield, East Sussex
TN22 1QQ England

Tel: +44 (0)1825 749494

www.naval-military-press.com
www.nmarchive.com

In reprinting in facsimile from the original, any imperfections are inevitably reproduced and the quality may fall short of modern type and cartographic standards.

PREFACE.

Our desire in presenting this little volume to the public, is to give a full and impartial statement of the late French operations on the River Min.

Having been eye-witnesses to the events herein-described, and having since had many opportunities of testing and correcting the numerous statements in circulation, we have rejected all that could not be fully verified by facts.

We wish to express our thanks to the naval and military authorities, who have furnished us with facts and data, and also to many correspondents who have so ably assisted us in our work.

The haste in which this volume has been compiled, and the many circumstances that have combined to retard its progress, must be our excuses for the faults which it undoubtedly contains.

That this, our maiden effort, may give satisfaction and reliable information, and meet with a generous approval from the public, is the sincere desire of

THE AUTHORS.

THE FRENCH AT FOOCHOW.

Chapter I.

FOOCHOW AND THE RIVER MIN.

Foochow, or more properly Fu-chow-foo, (Happy City) the scene of the recent French conquest, is situated in a picturesque position on the left bank of the river Min, twenty-six miles distant from the sea. Opened to foreign commerce by the treaty of 1842, the capital of the province of Fokien (or Fuh-keen) ranks to-day only second to Shanghai in commercial importance among the Chinese ports; and this in spite of obstacles, furnished by nature, such as harbour bars, narrow channels, etc.

The city contains about six hundred thousand inhabitants as near as one can estimate the population, and the city itself is of the better class, although retaining the national characteristics of dirt, smells, and disagreeable sights, without which you will never see a typical Chinese town. Five hills overlook Foochow, resting at their base on an undulating plain, which is divided into two sections, one Chinese (and thoroughly so), and the other containing the mercantile houses and residences of the "men of brain and business," that have borne hand in hand the Starry Banner of America and St. George's Cross of England to the antipodes, and combated successfully with native cunning, superstition, prejudice and bigotry, until that great civiliser of the world, intelligent trade, has been so firmly planted that revolutions shall not shake its grasp.

The Min is a river abounding in picturesque natural scenery, some parts of which would well repay a faithful reproduction. To enter it is necessary to cross a bar, which at high tide is covered by twenty-four feet of water. Inward, through narrow passes, opening into wider channels, then growing again to narrow roads, the observer looks upon paddy fields, dotted in the back-ground by the bamboo huts of the natives, who may be seen near by, working over their crops, their large sun hats bringing to mind early school days, when pictures contained in geographies and illustrated histories impressed the youthful mind more in the manner of Arabian tales than of substantial records of the world's mysterious corner. Still the steamer glides on, and we now look upon hills from small to great, all in a high state of cultivation, rising in green terraces from the still, calm river, upward to their very summits, and even there uplifting their fresh glad faces, clothed only with nature's complexion, in thankfulness to the God who cherishes and protects them.

And so, still moving, past hill and plain, we go through Mingan pass and come in full view of our long-looked-for haven, Pagoda Point. Making toward it, the Neptune of the ship, pointing to a small island, remarks, "Boys, that's Flat Island." Nothing interesting there, surely. No, not now; but in less than two weeks it will figure as a burial place for one of those Chinese sloops of war, now in sight, and riding the wave with her Imperial dragon waving so proudly at the gaff, and engaged in its everlasting attempt to swallow, so indicative of the Government it represents. Of course the chief point of interest at the anchorage, that is, to a stranger, is the object from which it takes its name. At the extreme upper part of Losing Island is a small mound or hill, upon whose summit rests the Pagoda. Looking from the river, immediately to the left, a square unpretentious building with the English flag floating above it, marks the home of the missionary. Clustered about and descending the hill to the water front, are numerous huts, and at the water's edge there are several substantial buildings, notable among which is the white square police station. A small house nestling in trees and bushes, has the flag of freedom floating over it, and is the agency of an American mercantile firm. Probably if we ascend the hill, to the Chinese street, we shall see the guileless natives pursuing their general toil, and also what is the staple product of this part of the country. Well, here is a Chinese shop; let us investigate its goods—Bass's Ale; Burke's Irish Whiskey; Hennessey's Brandy; Guinness' Stout and Cigars—and in the face of this some people dare hold that the Celestials cannot be civilised—a basket of rice, and some curious looking objects on a stick in the corner. We ask the name of the latter and the proprietor smiles, blandly significant, then answers, " No belong European chow-(food)."

The Pagoda is in shape and appearance similar to all of these curious buildings. An octagonal-shaped hollow shaft, rising between one hundred and one hundred and twenty feet; embellished at regular intervals on its sides by the usual cornices; and dome-shaped at its top, out of which a small straight pillar ascends for a few feet. According to the natives it was built very long ago, but its age they cannot determine. There is no doubt that it was erected anterior to the invasion of the Mongol Tartars, under the renowned Genghis Khan, in the early part of the thirteenth century. China has numerous Pagodas and temples; and although some of them may be in use for religious purposes, the majority only serve as curiosities, or landmarks, such as those on the banks of rivers and bays. It is estimated that at the present day, in Pekin and the vicinity fully eight thousand of them are standing, some of which are monuments of Chinese splendor; and there is no hamlet in the country, however small, that does not possess one at least of them, if even in miniature.

Opposite, across the river from the Pagoda, is the Custom House. It occupies a commanding position on the left shore, between the German Consulate on one side, and the residence of an Italian gentleman on the other. It is a large, white, square building, with a business-like aspect, facing the stream, a silent witness to scenes of blood and carnage, and an exemplification of the saying; "Wars may come, and wars may go, but trade rolls on for ever."

The Navy Yard and Dock being the objective points of attack by the French force, it will be necessary to place before our readers their location, value, and fitness for practical work.

Dividing Pagoda Point from the mainland is a small creek, above which stands the straggling village of Ma-moi extending back to the base of the hills, and is principally the abode of Chinese compradores who supply the ships at this place. And, beyond this, is the dock, which is of eastern structure, planked with wood, and similar in size and construction to those of Shanghai, with which it has about an equal capacity. This dock is surrounded by a high wall and in its vicinity stands a few brick buildings, engine or pump houses. Just beyond the dock, is a large coaling station, the contents of which were undermined by the Chinese before the battle, and of which fact the French were probably ignorant, as doubtless they would have exploded the mine when taking possession of the yard if they had been informed thereof. Next comes the Navy Yard and Arsenal which occupy an area of about ninety acres. It extends along the water for nearly the half of a mile, and has a long line of ways capable of accommodating large ships. The yard contains boiler shops, machine shops, foundries, etc., and in its offices may be found working drawings, with French headings. Around the yard runs the usual wall. This property was constructed under the direction of Frenchmen. Its estimated value to the Chinese government was fifty millions of dollars, including, of course, the dock. It has every appointment and facility that a wellfitted yard should have, and is capable of turning out ships that should be able to compete with those of some of the foreign nations at present trading with China. Before the engagement, two ships were on the stocks in the yard; one with the keel just laid, and the other so far advanced that her engines were being fitted to her. Two other new vessels had been built and launched, moored just in front of the yard, but were not thoroughly fitted. In the hasty preparations, howitzers were mounted upon these, that they might participate in the defence.

Immediately following the construction of the yard its management was given to Europeans—Frenchmen, and they continued in office for some time, doing good service, not only in building but in teaching to the natives the principles of work, building, etc., required in a place of its kind. These Europeans were much thought of at Pekin. M. Giquel, the first director of the Arsenal, was allowed a large European staff and many privileges. He and Gen. Gordon were the only two Europeans upon whom was conferred the "yellow riding jacket," the highest honour that the Imperial government of China can confer upon foreigners.

By degrees Chinese influence ousted European management. Not, however, until the native mind had mastered its problems and secured a good education in ship-building and the direction of affairs; enough, in fact, to carry on matters with their own ideas, and under the supervision of native minds. One tracing of the French is left—the language. The natives in the yard work by French plans, use French terms to designate their parts of work, and a large number of them, in fact all, with few exceptions, speak the French language.

Above the Navy Yard, the Min remains the same in a natural sense as below, being wider on the average. The hills and mountains can be seen reaching far into the country on either side, until the sight can follow their blue-crowned tops no further.

Chapter II.

"COMING EVENTS CAST THEIR SHADOWS BEFORE."

The United States steamer *Enterprise*, a vessel of the American squadron under the command of Commander Albert S. Barker, U. S. Navy, rode at anchor in the Woosung river near Shanghai, Sunday morning, July 10th, having been called to that place a few days before, from Yokohama, by rumours of war. Near by was the *Juniata*, under Commander Harrington, and up the stream, anchored off the U. S. Consulate, the *Trenton*, Capt. Phythian, having on board the flag and person of Rear Admiral John Lee Davis, U.S.N., Commandant of the United States forces in Asiatic waters.

On board the *Enterprise*, nothing unusual was occurring, the crew making prepartion for the weekly inspection by the commander; everything in its place, and a place for everything. Guns shining, muskets, cutlasses, and pistols, brightened, and an occasional interrogation as to whether the trouble would interfere with liberty to visit the shore. Outside of this perfect peace. And yet, in five minutes from receiving notice, this ship, in company with the others of her squadron, could have had boatloads of men, armed and equipped, on their way to the breach, prepared to protect foreign residents. Although the arrangements of Admiral Davis and his commanders had provided for every exigency, still neither officers nor men, though prepared, deemed such a contingency probable. That France and China would fight was questioned as much on board ship as ashore, and in the quarrel each side had its adherents. So the preparation and routine went on, and the Sabbath stillness prevailed. At ten o'clock, a signal from the *Trenton* calls Commander Barker to that ship. He goes and returns.

"Secure all boats for sea; we are going away." To-day! For where?—Nobody seems to know, until at last the rumour leaks out around the decks, that trouble, perhaps fighting, is anticipated at Foochow. But the *Monocacy* is there; further up the river than we can go. Yes, but we are to take the Admiral there to assume personal control. Besides, two ships are better than one in a case of this kind. So at thirty minutes past one, in the afternoon, having received Admiral Davis and some of his staff on board, we steam out of the river. Passing the Woosung forts, then the Red Buoy, we see the two French men-of-war *D'Estaing* and *Triomphante* laying calmly at anchor, to all intents and purposes peaceable enough. We shall meet them soon again, and in a different attitude—

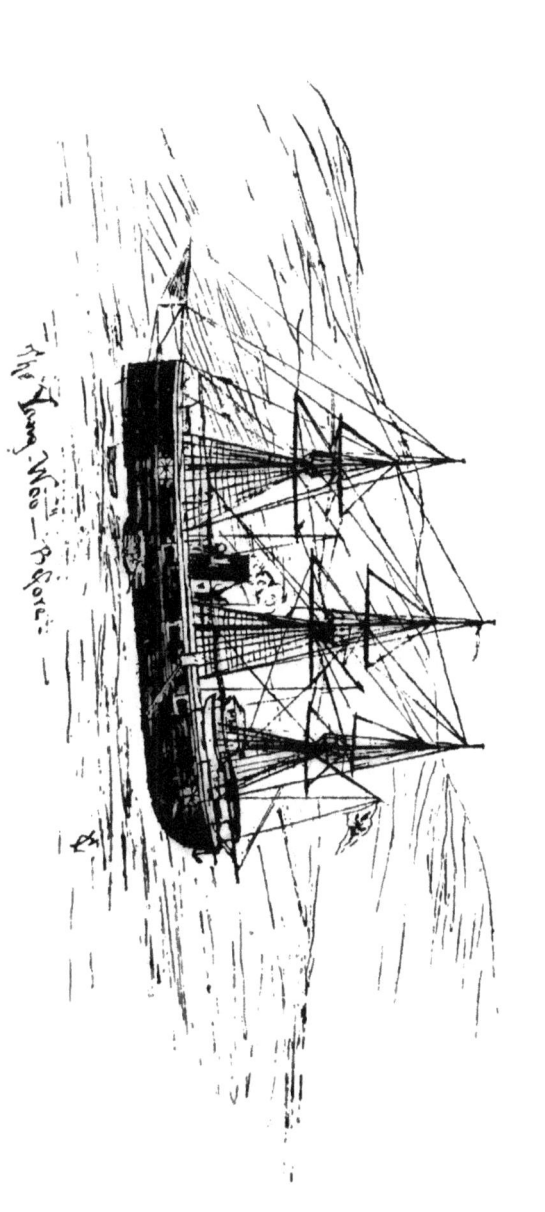

The Lung-Woo—Before.

belching death and destruction. The *Enterprise* reached Pagoda Anchorage, July 12th, a trifle after three o'clock. In the outer bay, near Sharp Peak, were sighted two French men-of-war, the *Galissoniere* and *Bayard*. At the anchorage, there were the following French war vessels; *Soane*, troop ship; *Duguay Trouin*, corvette; *Aspic*, *Lynx*, *Vipére*, and *Volta*, gunboats; the latter having on board one whose name was soon to be written in French history, more forcibly than in mere naval routine —Vice Admiral Courbet. These ships were prepared for battle, their upper masts being housed, revolving cannon in the tops, cables ready for slipping, and the men relieving each other at the guns by watches. Everything prepared for the grand finale enacted on that Saturday so fatal to China.

Besides these ships, there were in the river two vessels of H.M.'s squadron, viz., *Champion* and *Sapphire*. Also three merchant barques the *Sin Kolga*, *Batavia*, and *Guiding Star*; steamers *Taku*, *Glenfinlas*, and *Mary Austin*. A fleet of Chinese war ships were anchored in defensive order, leading from the Custom House to above the Navy Yard:—the *Yang Woo*, flagship; *Yang-Pao*, *Chun-hing*, *Chun-shing*, *Fuh-shing*, *Yee-sing*, *Foo-poo*, *Chi-an*, *Fei-Yuen*, *Chin-Wei*, and *Fuh-sing*. Thirteen war junks, armed with smooth bore cannon, guarded the creek just around the Pagoda bend, and innumerable fire-rafts, filled with explosives, were expected to spread destruction among the ships of the French. The U.S.S. *Monocacy*, under Francis J. Higginson, Commander, U.S. Navy, was at anchor off the city of Foochow, and to her Admiral Davis transferred his flag, soon after arriving. H.M.'s *Merlin* lay near the *Monocacy*, and the presence of these two vessels gave foreigners a sense of relief from probable trouble. Immediately on our arrival rumours of the most wild and varied kind reached us. The French were to open fire at sunrise. Torpedoes had been planted by both sides under each opposing ship. And so they flew about, making the situation such that, if true, an instant would have completed the battle and both fleets have disappeared in smoke. Day after day came and went with ensuing quietness, and the situation remained the same, save that the soldiers ashore might be seen strengthening their defences, over which (with the exception of those at the Pagoda) floated banners and streamers enough to have supplied a field division of European troops. "Braves" from all near provinces were reported as encamped behind the different hills, but if so they stayed there as nothing could be seen to verify their presence. The Chinese and French fleets maintained their positions, each covered by the guns of the other, and in perfect condition to fight.

August 15th, the French corvette *Villars* arrived from the South. The following day being the birthday of H.I.M. the Emperor of China, all ships in the river (French included) dressed with flags at the mastheads, in honor of the occasion. In the afternoon, the *Villars* left, and the ram corvette *D'Estaing* arrived. The next day H.M.S. *Vigilant* arrived and received Vice-Admiral Dowell and his flag. During the day the large cruiser *Duguay Trouin* went out, returning within twenty-four hours, accompanied by the *Villars*, passing the small ram *Lynx* going out through Mingan pass. The latter returned to her station on the morning of the twenty-first. There is no doubt that these vessels proceeded below the forts for the purpose of replenishing their supplies. During these movements the steamer *Woosung* arrived and took up a position near the other merchant steamers.

August 20th, seemingly well-founded rumours reached us that the decisive day had arrived, and that before darkness came the battle would either have been finished, or well under progress. Perhaps this may have been the arrangement, but if so there never was a better exemplification of man proposing and a higher power interposing. A sudden gale sprang into existence in the early morning, and soon had assumed the proportions of nearly a typhoon. The wind whistled, like the screech of a boatswain's pipe, and the rain descended in sheety torrents, thoroughly drenching those whom duty called to its exposure. It increased in violence during the day, so much so that the vessels of H.M.'s squadron were seen to send down their upper yards and topgallant masts. All wandering sampans hied themselves to the friendly shelter of the different creeks, while no more ventured on the bosom of the angry river. The day following brought in its early part no abatement of the storm. All the ships were under only lower yards and masts, the wind still howling, the rain still beating, and the river lashed to a yellow foam, giving the different vessels a motion nearly similar to that at sea. " I pity the poor fellows outside in such a storm as this " was the remark of many an old sailor.

And still with all this our friend Rumour still survives, and makes his daily round of the ship. " Fighting will begin at three o'clock to-day, at the changing of the tide." This on the best of authority !—Oh ! this best of authority ! Why cannot someone start news on *no* authority ? Best authority has failed us so often that a change might produce truth—that quality, such a stranger in all parts, that when it visits a place we know not whether its intention is for good or evil, and hesitate in the welcome.

At three o'clock movements among the fleets seemed to confirm the rumor of the morning. The Chinese vessels near the Custom House got up anchor and steamed about the harbor, sometimes very close to the French ships. One of them in particular, nearly struck the bowsprit of the *Duguay Trouin*, so close did she pass. The French fleet stayed at anchor, apparently unconcerned, with the exception of the *Duguay Trouin* and *D'Estaing*, both of which were seen to be on the move and seemingly alert for anything that might occur We believed at the time that it was the intention of these Chinamen to manœuvre for the purpose of seeing whether the French intended to stop their exit from the harbor ; and seeing the opposing rams prepared to prevent any trial of the sort, they went quietly back to their moorings, and matters once more assumed a state of quiescence.

The 22nd opened with a better prospect. The rain still decended in heavy showers, but the wind had moderated to a considerable extent. Between nine and ten o'clock in the morning, the English and American war ships, lowered boats, and filling them with men, armed with Gatling guns, howitzers, muskets, pistols, cutlasses etc., and well supplied with ammunition, despatched them to Foochow settlement, the former to reinforce the crew of H.M.S. *Merlin*, and the latter that of the U.S.S. *Monocacy*. This certainly looked like business, and the hurried departure of the men through the rain and mist started many a theory about the decks. In the morning the troop ship *Soane* left the river. Nothing again to-day. Junks and sampans gliding along on their course, and all around unchanged; our compradore comes aboard in the afternoon and wants a general settlement. "Frenchman he fight sure to-morrow." Yes, but he has told us this so often. This time, however, he persists in wanting his bills paid, as he is assured to-morrow may be too late, and he wishes to be in the interior when the fighting begins. So accounts are closed and he departs for his place of security. It is evident from the arrangements made by all, that the feeling is strengthening into conviction that matters are assuming a more business-like aspect, and that we shall not pass many more days of intense expectation without a realisation of some sort, substantial or otherwise. Night comes on dark and gloomy, a fitting prelude to the morrow. Not a sound can be heard on the river except perhaps the splash or creak of an oar in an occasional passing sampan. The whole bay is enveloped in blackness, only the indicating lights of the different steamers and ships relieving the scene. At about eight o'clock the French squadron illumines the prospect, by flashing their electric and calcium lights about the harbor. Everything peaceful except on shore, where the Chinamen, with the quietness of the dead, are working like beavers, especially at the fort on Pagoda point, near the water front. Here an endless chain of men can be seen running between fort and rear of the hill. What they are carrying cannot be ascertained, but that black ram in the stream is evidently interested for she keeps the place flooded in a blaze of light, which is only occasionally withdrawn, for a moment's gaze at some other object on river or on shore, entitled to suspicion.

And so the light keeps moving, flashing now on houses that shall be ruins ere the sun sets once more. On men, that shall be torn part from part, beyond all semblance of manhood. On ships, made to ride the sea, that shall be perforated, battered, destroyed, and sunk to the bottom of the element they were made to conquer;

and on hills that shall be plowed with instruments strange to agriculture, and sown with seed too hard and solid to fertilize.

At midnight all is silent. On these ships sleep brave strong men knowing they must fight, but for whose honour or for what cause or principle, they, the most interested, are ignorant. What pictures float through the dreams of these Asiatic slumberers? Who can tell? Of their humble home, perhaps, with visions of cherished wife, and lisping babe clinging about their knees, the hope of a future generation;—for doubt not that these are human and love their offspring. And now again his wife in some familiar picture smiling lovingly upon him. That smile to-morrow shall change to weeping moans and tears of anguish. Sleep on then, man! To-morrow thou shalt awake, but only to feel the pangs and tortures of death, and enter upon a longer sleep, from which thou shalt again awake and meet thine enemy in another long promised field, where there shall be no combating of opposing forces, no dissension, only Judgment.

Chapter III.

THE BATTLE OF MA-MOI.

The early dawn of Saturday the 23rd of August foretold a day of surpassing loveliness and ineffable calm. Cloudlessly the sun rose from behind the eastern hills, tipping their lofty summits with gold, and making the face of nature resplendent with his brilliant rays. Serene, placid, unruffled, rolled on the swift current of the river Min, so soon to be the bearer of the thrilling tidings and the silent witnesses that would so eloquently testify to the complete destruction of China's fleet, ere the breaking day closed in slumbering night. Early in the morning, the Consuls, foreign residents, and the various men-of-war and other non-combatant vessels in the harbor, received official notice from Admiral Courbet, that he intended toop en fire upon the Chinese fleet, and bombard the forts and government property on shore, at noon of that day. The morning was passed on board the French vessels in making the final preparations for the deadly struggle so soon to be decided, but the Chinese seemed unaware of their approaching danger, and remained entirely inactive. The vertical rays of the blazing sun pouring down from a cloudless sky, with not a breath of air stirring, combined to make the suspense of the forenoon thrilling to us, who were to be only spectators of the tragedy about to be enacted. What must it have been to those who stood at their guns, without shade or protection of any kind from the torrid heat, chafing with an intense desire approaching almost to madness, to give utterance to their impacable hatred in fire and smoke and deadly shell? The morning hours rolled slowly by. From eleven till noon was to many present the longest hour ever experienced. It is said that the hours pass all too rapidly, to the condemned one waiting for certain death; but the flight of time is slow indeed; the many revolving wheels of its progression are clogged by some mysterious agency; the minutes seem hours, the hours become days to the spectator awaiting the signal to be made which shall bring a probable death to others. For some minutes previous to the appointed hour of noon, so complete was the silence that reigned over the harbor, that the faintest sound was audible from the far off vessels and Navy Yard of the Chinese. Every one stood gasping, staring with interest at some small object far up the river, the centre of the French fleet and cynosure of all eyes, the gunboat *Lynx*.

Eight bells were struck on board the merchant vessels, on the English men-of-war, on the steamers and sailing ships far up the river, on the Chinese men-of-war, on went the death knell. At last the harbinger of woe was heard to chime from the bell of the *Lynx*. No gun was fired, no tongue of flame, puff of smoke and quicker report proclaimed the work of destruction begun. The sighs of relief came down the river like a breeze! Respite for a short while yet,—all too brief, poor celestials! This delay was unaccountable.

At fifty-two minutes past one, a large man-of-war was discovered standing up the river. No sooner had she come plainly to view, and her name—the *Triomphante*—and nationality became apparent, than we knew intuitively that the arrival of this vessel was for some esoteric reason what the French had been waiting for. Coming in sight of the Flagship, numbers were rapidly exchanged, and signals made. A flash of fire, a puff of smoke, and the ominous report of a Hotchkiss gun from the maintop of the *Lynx*, boomed forth death and destruction to the navy of the Flowery Land (1h. 56m. 13s. p.m.) So rapid was the reply from the Chinese sloop *Ching Wai*, lying inshore abreast of the Custom House, levelled at the hull of the *D'Estaing*, that the reports reached us simultaneously. Instantly fire and smoke belched forth from every iron mouth. The contending fleets were enveloped in a dense cloud, and the report that came down the river was indescribably terrific, making the hills reverberate and tremble to their very foundations. Twenty-seven seconds after the firing of the signal gun, (1h. 56m. 40s.) a tremendous explosion was heard in the direction of the Navy Yard. The smoke clearing away it was seen that the *Yang-woo*, the Chinese flagship, had been blown up by a torpedo boat of the enemy. Leaving the protecting sides of the *Volta* at a preconcerted signal, rapidly darting in under cover of the smoke occasioned by the firing of the guns of the *Yang-woo*, and laying the engine of destruction under the stern of the ill-fated ship, which instantly exploded, the Torpilleur, number 45, accomplished its work and destroyed the largest and most imposing ship of the Chinese.

The cannonading kept up on both sides was terrific. The forts on shore, especially the water battery on Pagoda island, doing excellent service, kept the French vessels on the right busy, while the four Chinese ships in front and above the Custom House engaged the attention of the *D'Estaing*, *Duguay Trouin* and *Villars* on the left. The *Volta* (flagship), followed by the *Vipére*, *Aspic*, and *Lynx*, moved up the river, engaging the enemy in that direction and bombarding the Navy Yard and Arsenal. Upon seeing the foe rounding the point, bent upon blood and destruction, the crew of the Chinese brigantine *Foo-Poo* were so terrified that they obtained possession of the vessel and ran her upon the bank, deserting immediately, and making all haste to seek a shelter more secure among the hills.

Meanwhile the grandest scene of this most dire tragedy was being enacted. The *Triomphante*, in all the stately majesty of strength, was steaming slowly up the river. Not a sound to be heard from the decks covered with men standing at their quarters, eager to send destructive heralds of iron shell into the enemy's vessels to tell of their approach. When distant a little over a mile from the scene of action, and nearly abreast the U.S.S. *Enterprise*, those on board that vessel could have distinctly heard the order given by the Captain on the bridge of the *Triomphante* to clear away and load the long bow chaser. Without noise, without confusion this was done. The gun sighted and fired. The shell sped on its rapid flight toward the upper forts on Pagoda Island. Now the Chinese realised that they had to look out for an attack from the enemy in the rear. The order was again given from the bridge of the *Triomphante*, and the gun once more loaded and fired, this time with a very different result. The shot stricking the *Ching-wai* in the stern, sweeping the decks and passing out under the bowsprit, seemed to lift the unfortunate vessel almost entirely out of the water, so great was the concussion occasioned by the huge projectile. This was the signal for one of the most disgraceful incidents that ever happened, even in the annals of the *Chinese* Navy. The cowardly crew deserted their guns, and jumping into the boats, lowered them and pulled away from the ship. Those who were unable to obtain seats in the boats, threw themselves overboard, and swam to the shore. The captain, first lieutenant, and the few loyal ones remaining on board, continued to bravely work the guns; and be it said eternally to their credit found time to discharge their lee broadside at the dastardly runaways, sinking two of the boats freighted with these unnatural wretches. After fighting for some few moments, with his remnant of a crew, the courageous commander endeavoured to get his now rapidly sinking vessel alongside his nearest anta-

Sinking of the Chung-Wai

gonist, the *D'Estaing*, evidently with the intention of blowing his own and the enemy's ship into limbo together; his patriotic ardor (a quality very rare among his nation) counting it small loss to sacrifice his own life, so that he might be the cause of sending so many of his hated foes to the region of kingdom come. This was not to be; a broadside from the *Villars* hulled the *Ching Wai* so severely that it was now a matter of only a few moments before she must go down. At the same time fire broke out forward, and several rapid explosions were heard, as from small arm ammunition that had been left around the decks. With all the characteristic bravery that one would expect from such a noble resistance, the captain reserved one loaded gun till the last moment, and then as the battered and shot-rent ship gave the last mournful roll, he pulled the lock-string and sent hissing on its errand of hate the last farewell of the unfortunate *Ching Wai*. An episode such as the foregoing is unprecedented in the records of the most ancient navy of the world, both for the extreme cowardice displayed on the one hand, and at the same time for the superhuman efforts and extraordinary bravery manifested on the other.

The valiant and plucky conduct of this commander is in marked contrast to that of two others in command, one of whom left his ship immediately after the firing of the first broadside, the crew setting fire to the vessel, and following his example; and the other, who fought his ship for about fifteen minutes, till it caught fire *forward*, then deserting his post, *had his gig lowered* and went ashore. The crew immediately availed themselves of this grand opportunity to obtain liberty, and in the exuberance of their joy at having obtained this tacit permission to visit the shore, they did not, like their gallant commander, wait to lower the boats, but actually jumped overboard and swam to the beach, leaving their ship to drift down the stream in flames, soon to explode and become a thing of the past! Many of these fainthearted wretches suffered the ignominious death that their dishonorable and cowardly conduct so richly merited; and it is to be hoped that those who escaped from the shell of the enemy, and from drowning in the river, may have their deeds of this day published far and wide, and that they may meet with the universal reproach which they so richly deserve, and be handed down to posterity covered with perpetual dishonor.

The *Triomphante* steamed slowly, majestically on; not the least sign or hurry or confusion was visible among those who crowded her decks, waiting and anxious to take part in a few minutes in the general engagement. There being no breeze to carry away the dense smoke, the thickest of the action was hidden from view of the spectators down the river, but for some thirty minutes the firing was terrific.

At eight minutes after two o'clock, one of the small Chinese gunboats came around Pagoda point, from the direction of the Navy Yard. The large thirty-five ton gun was fired once at the mammoth ram *Duguay Trouin*; the projectile missed its mark and buried itself hissing and spluttering in the hills beyond. In response, apparently every gun in the enemy's fleet was levelled at the hull of their puny but audacious antagonist. The shock of the volley of shells was so great that it stopped the headway of the gunboat and seemed to drive her backwards. For fully two minutes she remained above the water, a helpless target for the pitiless guns of the enemy. A shot entered her magazine, a loud explosion was heard, and with one headlong dive the gunboat disappeared from view, just ahead of the s.s. *Glenfinlas*, beneath the waters of the river Min. At twenty-five minutes past two, the mine laid by the Chinese under the docks at the Navy Yard was exploded by the French ships. Twenty minutes after a Chinese sloop of war, emerging from the smoke of the action, drifted down the river in flames, sinking with colors flying, about two miles below the Custom House. Another sloop came down, a few minutes later, also on fire, but with colors down, grounding on Flat Island. Two hours later the fire reached the magazine, and the vessel blew up into a thousand fragments. At thirty minutes after three, another Chinese sloop, in flames, with French colors hoisted half way up at the mizzen, drifted slowly down, on her way fouling the s.s. *Taku*, which, with the loss of an anchor, barely escaped being set on fire by the passing vessel. This one shared the same fate as the others in stranding and being ultimately blown up by the ignition of the powder in her magazine. As this mass of flame and heat was passing, we observed several natives clinging to the rudder shaft under the stern. One was terribly wounded, his thigh being shot close off. All the assistance possible was rendered to these unfortunate victims by the English and American steam launches, but many perished from drowning before they could be picked up.

About four o'clock the firing became less rapid and spirited, but the French continued to keep up a slow and regular fire at the forts on shore, which were still making a feeble resistance. About this time fire rafts and junks laden with explosive and inflammable material, such as gunpowder, kerosene oil, sulphur, etc., began to come down with the tide. One of these dangerous engines of war got athwart of the hawser of the barque *Sin Kolga*, but was hauled off by the steam launches, without doing much damage. At six o'clock, the French launches, armed with machine guns, opened a brisk fire on a number of junks anchored in a creek running between Losing Island and the mainland. The men-of-war not engaged in covering this party with their guns, were engaged in destroying the fire rafts and burning junks which were coming down the river three and four at a time. About thirty minutes past seven, a Chinese gunboat came around Pagoda point in flames. The French opened fire with their Hotchkiss and great guns, endeavouring to sink the dangerous craft, but the shell only caused showers of sparks and tongues of flame to shoot up from the burning vessel, which presently drifted down, and broke in two across the bows of the *Glenfinlas*.

From the hottest of the fight, through the densest smoke, the French torpedo boat, number 45, came down the river toward the U. S. S. *Enterprise*, and lay just off to the port, and then to the starboard side of that vessel. Those in the tops and rigging of the *Enterprise*, who found time to turn their eyes from the tragic spectacle up the river, and to look down upon the grey mite of a Torpilleur lying alongside, were surely surprised that so small an object could, when armed with its terrible torpedoes, carry such complete destruction to the great Leviathans of the deep. The monstrous ships of the present age, the floating cities, carrying more souls from shore to shore than many of the ancient Greek states contained, are entirely at the mercy of these pigmy torpedo boats.

It was evident that the boat had been in the thickest of the fight. The crew of eight men, stripped to the waist, were bespattered with blood from head to foot. One man had his left arm bandaged to above the elbow, and the officer in command was not to be seen. To describe the physique of these men is beyond my power. Swarthy black-bearded Sons of Collus and Terra, bleeding and soul begrimmed, as if fresh from forging the thunder bolts of Almighty Jove, in the depths below, panting with rage and dissappointment, like bloodhounds torn from their prey; breathing forth words of fire, like the condemned hurled into the infernal abyss; preternatural in appearance, superhuman in energy and strength, ready at the slightest hint, at the most feeble gesture of their disabled commander, to rush headlong into fire and smoke, carnage, death, and eternity. One of this crew of picked volunteers was a boy of scarce eighteen years of age. The steam launch of the *Enterprise* was out rendering assistance to the wounded and drowning of both sides, and the officer in charge, seeing that the torpedo boat was evidently in distress, run the launch alongside and enquired what was the matter. The boatswain, who spoke good English, said that their commander had been wounded, and was lying below in the pilot house. He then went and carefully assisted the wounded man on deck. Pale and bloodstained, with a bandage over his eye, stood the hero of the day, the destroyer of the largest ship of the enemy. The apothecary of the *Enterprise* went to him, examined and dressed his wound, and gave him all the relief possible in such a place or under such circumstances. He proposed that both wounded men should be taken on board the American ship, but the officer politely refused, saying that he could not leave his command, and the sailor in stronger and more expressive terms, assured his companion, the boatswain, who acted as interpeter, that he would never forsake his commander, or boat, as long as the one lived, or the other floated. Sweet, yet strong, must be the power of that chain which so fascinates mankind at times, that they risk everything, and dearest life itself, to obtain " the bubble reputation even in the cannon's mouth."

During and subsquent to the engagement, the steam launches were kept busily engaged in rescuing the Chinamen that came floating down, seven and eight together, clinging to fragments of masts and spars, and the wreckage that covered the surface of the water. Among the victims that went floating down with the tide, unrescued, a large black dog from the *Yang-woo*, swimming bravely and making every effort to reach the shore, and a rooster floating on a log of wood, the most forlorn, dejected, and thoroughly disgusted looking bird it is possible to imagine.

Chapter IV.

DAYS FOLLOWING.

After the bombardment on the water had ceased, and the firing from the forts on shore become considerably less spirited, numerous fires broke out in the direction of the Navy Yard and Arsenal, spreading to an alarming extent. Soon the tongues of flame lit up the heavens with a lurid glare that was visible for miles in every direction. The numerous and loud reports of explosions, could be heard for a great distance, and kept the many and anxious watchers at Foochow, both on the ships and shore, on the *qui vive*, and gave rise to manifold conjectures as to their cause. To add to the glare from the burning Arsenal and villages, which made the blackest hour of midnight as bright as day, a Chinese gunboat drifted down the river in flames, and presently blowing up scattered a shower of sparks far and wide, giving the river the appearance of one mass of fire.

The ever watchful victors kept up a desultory fire

all night until four o'clock on the morning of the 24th when, having discovered something suspicious with their powerful search lights, they opened a brisk fire with machine and great guns, upon Losing Island and sent out steam launches to reconnoitre. The daydawn of Sunday presented a mournful spectacle. The gallant ships of yesterday no longer floated on the placid bosom of the River Min; the yellow ensign, with sacred dragon, no more spread its folds to the breeze; death and destruction, the sad monuments alike of human power and human frailty, alone were there on that quiet Sabbath morning, to account for the loss of the Chinese fleet. A little before eight o'clock, several junks drifted down the river in flames. At thirty-five minutes past ten, the *Voltc*, *Aspic* and *Lynx*, moved up the river towards the dockyard. Soon after heavy firing occurred, and a party of armed men were sent from the *Duguay Trouin*, to land at the mouth of a small creek above the Custom House.

In the early part of the afternoon, the French performed the last mournful ceremonies due to those who had perished on the previous day, fighting for the beloved tricolor that has so often waved victorious over scenes of blood and carnage, both on land and sea. The colours of all vessels in the harbour were half-masted while the hardy patriots were being interred in foreign soil far, far away from the vineclad hills and sunny slopes of *La Belle France!* Seven small mounds of earth, hastily thrown up, mark the last resting places of a like number of French sailors, victims of the world's necessity—war. During the afternoon the three gunboats off the dock-yard kept up a slow regular fire, and five large and heavy explosions occurred in the direction of the dropping shells. Heavy firing was heard down the river about this time, from the guns of the French man-of-war, *La Galissoniére*, bombarding the lower forts. Towards six o'clock the firing ceased, the French ships came back to their former anchorage, night came on apace, and threw her dusky wings in folds of deepest black over the now peaceful scene, occasionally lit up by a lurid flicker from expiring embers of the afternoon fires. Save for the regular chimes from the bells, and the hail passed by the watchful sentries on post, as the hours rolled slowly on, the harbour was like

the abode of the departed, so quiet, so peaceful, so sure were
the victors of the completeness of their conquest, that they
failed to keep their usual vigilant look-out with the calcium
lights.

During the engagement of Sunday afternoon, a spent
shell came on the hills, from the angular fire of the French
directed at the dock-yard, and passed whizzing and whist-
ling between the main and mizzen-masts of the *Enterprise*,
striking the water about a hundred yards on the opposite
side. The small crowd assembled on the poop for some
unaccountable reason ducked their heads and inhaled very
rapidly an immense quantity of the surrounding atmosphere,
exhaling it again in the form of a series of expressive inter-
jections culminating in expletives. The eloquent pause in
the conversation, caused by the rapid transit of the French
projectile, was first broken by the commander, who gave the
order to get underway. To discourse in a learned manner,
in scientific terms, upon the sudden exhaustion occasioned
by the rapid progression of a solid body through the atmosphere, would be out of place here, nor would it be appro-
priate to moralize on the indisputable fact that corporeal
absence is preferable to mental presence in episodes like the
above.

Monday, the 25th, was ushered in by long and
heavy firing from the machine guns of the French, in the
direction of the Custom House. At seven o'clock a large
landing party left the ships, covered by the guns of the fleet,
landing at the foot of the Pagoda on Losing Island. They
proceeded to raze the earth works and those portions of the
forts left standing, and returned to their vessels about
eleven.

At half-past twelve Admiral Courbet visited the
foreign men-of-war in the harbour. Ten minutes later the
French fleet got underway and steamed down the river, the
Admiral joining his ship, now the mammoth *Duguay Trouin*,
as she passed the U.S.S. *Enterprise*. As it is possibly the
last time we shall see these heroes together we will review
them in passing.

First the stately and majestic *Triomphante*, the king
of ships. Conscious of unknown power, of untold strength,
sensible of great destruction effected, victory achieved, of
laurels won. Plough on, brave ship, thy way to fresh

glory and new honour; may the Gods of War be seated ever on thy prow. *Duguay Trouin*, a giant among thy kind, a mammoth ship. Thou and the pigmy *Torpilleur* thou hast under thy protecting wing have become notorious indeed. Thy work was well done *Volta*, into the thickest of the fight went the flag of chief command and victory at thy fore-royal mast-head. The honour be all thine of bearing the head that planned and directed the conquering heroes of Saturday. *D'Estaing*, familiar form, as terrible in war as friendly in peace. Fresh honour awaits thee! The "Chinois" shall feel thy fangs yet again. *Vipère* and *Aspic*, well named, sharp-stinging, snake-like, gliding. Let thine enemies beware! *Villars*, seen oft before in peaceful times. Formosa knows thee well; Foochow has heard of thee. Go on thy way and gather new laurels to thine already crowded brow. *Lynx!* never was one more aptly fitted with a name. Prowling, sly, crafty, thy long lean body glides stealthily into the very midst of the unsuspecting foe; fire flashes from thy mouth, and the signal of death to thousands has gone forth from thy lips! The two torpedo boats were towing alongside the *Duguay Trouin* and *D'Estaing*. The squadron came to anchor about three miles down the river.

Several times during the afternoon the reports of heavy guns were heard toward the river mouth, from the French vessels stationed there to guard the approaches. The fleet on the way down passed the s.s. *China*, flying the German flag and standing up the river towards the Pagoda Anchorage. This vessel was laden with arms and ammunition for the Chinese Government, and had that morning landed seven hundred soldiers from Swatow, at Sharp Peak, under cover of the friendly forts.

At five o'clock the squadron came to anchor just below Spiteful Island, and commenced to casually bombard the Mingan forts at the head of the pass. The Chinese were unable to reply from the greater number of their guns as they were set in solid masonry and trained to fire down the river only. Such defenses as these can be attained with impunity from either side, or the rear, or in fact from any point outside of the fixed line of fire.

Half an hour later, a detachment of men with machine guns were landed on the left bank of the river, and at the same time the *Lynx* steamed down to cover them with her guns. After an hour's work on shore, the landing party returned to their ships, and the French ceased firing with the exception of an occasional gun; once more night came to the rescue, and wrapped in her kindly embrace the affrighted and dispersed regiments of the "Emperor of the Flower Land."

We will seize the present opportunity while the French are still sleeping, to reckon up the losses in killed, wounded, etc., sustained by them and their antagonists, since the commencement of the engagement on Saturday last. The first shot fired from the bow gun of the *Yang-woo*, struck the pilot of the flagship *Volta*, Capt. Thomas, of Shanghai, killing him instantly. Shortly after, the vessel received a shot about three inches above the water line, on the starboard side, which passed through her, killing six powder passers on the berth deck. A quarter-master of this vessel was killed, later on. The *Duquay Trouin* and *Villars* were both struck, but the visible external damage sustained was so slight that none of the crew could have been killed, and very few, if any, injured.

Probably many were severely wounded and some perhaps killed during the shore engagements of Sunday and Monday, as the firing, expecially on the first day, was very brisk and the enemy maintained their positions for some time.

From all the information I can gather, I estimate the French loss in killed at twelve men, and their pecuniary losses at a merely nominal sum. The Chinese have a very different account to show, their casualties and losses in killed amounting to nearly three thousand, and in money to fifteen millions of dollars. There were two hundred and seventy men on board the *Yang-woo*, at the time of the explosion; fifteen of them including Captain, Staff-commander and Sub-Lieutenant, it is reported, were saved. This is hardly likely, as the force of the explosion was so great that from mutilated bodies which have since been found on the roofs of the houses in the village of Ma-moi, distant nearly a mile from where the *Yang-woo* was anchored, and identified as the remains of men that were stationed on the flagship at the time of the disaster.

If the force imparted by the bursting of the torpedo was so terrific, it is very probable that the only persons who were saved from this unfortunate ship were the lucky few, about six in number, who were made aware of their danger, and jumped overboard, preferring to trust themselves to the mercy of the water, and chance escape from the Hotchkiss shells, falling thick as hail around them, than to making a rapid ascent in the air, and descending with even increasing velocity to perhaps alight on some hard substance. The alternative was not pleasant. The complement of the *Ching-Wai* was slightly over one hundred men ; some of these saved themselves by flight, but more than half must have been slain by the terrible hail from the enemy's machine guns, and the final broadside from the *Villars*. The brave commander and his second officer were killed. One sloop carrying one hundred and fifty men, was blown to pieces, and two gunboats, with thirty to forty men each, were sunk before their crews had time to make their escape. The greater part of these were sent in sections to swell the ranks of " the great majority."

As we have already seen, the crew of the brigantine *Foo-Poo* escaped in their successful endeavors to exemplify the axiom that " discretion is the better part of valor." Five other sloops, with crews ranging in number from one hundred to one hundred and forty men each, and thirteen junks having complements of not less than forty, have yet to be accounted for, before the point of complete destruction is reached. When the engagements and explosions on shore and in the dockyard have been taken into consideration, the loss in killed on the side of the conquered could not have been much less than the above estimate of three thousand. The native authorities on shore, admit having lost more than half of the number. So, allowing for Chinese artifice and their habit of disguising the real facts, if they happen in any way to be detrimental to the government, I consider the estimate as being under rather than over the amount slain.

For many days after the action, dead bodies in all stages of decomposition, and some mutilated and contorted beyond human recognition, were thick upon the river; drifting up and down with the coming and out-going tides. The stench was unbearable. We will now close the chapter with a short review of what remains to China after the engagement which began with Saturday.

Coming down the river, from the Foochow settlement; nothing is seen damaged until about half-way to the anchorage, where we discover the *Foo-Poo*, with broken back, brought up here and deserted by her crew during the engagement. The Chinese authorities will endeavour to get this ship from the beach for the purposes of repair. When deserted she was left with her head pointing down stream, but since then the tides have changed her position, so that she rests forming an angle with the small pagoda on the opposite bank. Just below this pagoda is encamped a large party of soldiers. Where the abandoned ship is the Chinese have erected river barriers, with foundations of rock and stone, overlaid by logs and various like material. From each side of the river, junks laden with stone, and sand in bags, have been sunk, and these, with the barriers, have effectually prevented the passage of ships. At high water parts of them are covered, but at low water the whole is distinguishable, and a narrow channel, fit only for the egress of a small junk, or a steam launch, finishes the only mode of communication between Foochow and the Anchorage. Just below these barriers, near the camp of the soldiers, another obstruction has been commenced and is progressing with speed. From this down to the Navy Yard, no destruction is visible, with the exception of stray shot (mostly from Hotchkiss guns) having struck in some of the villages. Approaching the yard one would imagine the damage done hardly enough for such a fire. A portion of the wall about the coal yard, and the same at the dock, is the only visible evidence of battle, but on landing a different scene presents itself to view. Destruction is on every side. The coal-yard remains about the same, with the above exception, although no doubt a heavy weight of French iron is mingled with the carbon and is visible in the shape of an occasional small shot. The machine shops are perforated and battered in an extraordinary manner. The tall chimney which marked their position, and was also a guide to the river pilots, withstood the conflagration of Saturday night and Sunday morning, but in the afternoon it fell in ruins. The machinery is twisted and bent out of shape, and probably of no more use. The boiler shop is in the same condition. The engine and pump houses were not struck by any large shot, but the Hotchkiss balls perforated them and damaged the interior to great extent. Along the front of the yard is a quantity of wreckage.

Our readers may remember the two ships on the stocks. Of these, the one nearest completion was totally destroyed, while the other was left untouched; of the two completed ships one was left intact with the exception of small shot in her spars and masts, and the other was burnt to the water's edge. Strewn along the beach are rafters, masts, and other belongings of the numerous junks that were destroyed, the larger part of their timbers floating seaward.

At Pagoda point there is a considerable evidence of severe fighting; as is only natural, for here the larger guns of the French were brought to play. Junks smashed, and huddled together, form an incongruous mass, though in some rotation, at a short distance from the shore, and in their midst the smoke-stack of a gunboat points to the sky. The fire on board this craft evidently extended to her bunkers, for she blazed for twelve days after the battle. On her stern may yet be seen a gun, probably a sixty pounder. The hull of the unfortunate *Yang-woo* is still visible. The damage sustained is not so great as a spectator of the terrific explosion would have been led to expect.

On the island many houses are perforated with shot— mostly Hotchkiss. The part facing up the river did not sustain much damage, but the other side, containing the forts, looks as if a pickaxe and crowbar brigade had been at work there. The lower fort was composed of seven solid columns of masonry, of which only three remain, the rest having crumbled to dust. Intending to give you an example of the precision with which the French fired, this fort may serve as an example. Of these columns one was used as a tide-mark by the pilots, and although between two others, not distant five feet from either, it was not injured in the slightest manner, while the two spoken of as being

on either side were levelled. The fort at the upper part of the hill was battered beyond recognition. In each of these forts remained two guns after the French had left the river, which have since been removed by the Chinese, although probably spiked by the French landing party of Monday morning. Directly off the Pagoda, in the direction of the Custom House, an Alphabetical gunboat was sunk, but of her nothing can be seen.

On the Custom House side the building itself was struck on the roof facing the river, by a large shot, and the side looking down the river shows many marks of the work of machine guns. Nothing else about here bears signs of injury but the hills, whose sides present numerous holes not in them before the bombardment.

Just below this the gallant *Ching Wai* showed her masts and spars above water for several days, but is now completely hidden from sight. Considerably lower down is visible the stern and mizzen-mast of a sloop, and looters may be seen at work removing anything within reach that is of value, even to the charred shrouds. On Flat Island rests the bare hull of another of the Chinese ships. The villages on the other side sustained little damage, only a few spent shells having entered them.

For a few days after the battle, the shores of the islands hereabouts were covered with wood, spars, plaited cane shields and other work, wooden eyes from the junks, straw hats and mats, pikes, everything in fact to be found in a Chinese man-of-war or war junk.

Chapter V.

MINGAN AND KIMPAI.

Before following the motions of the French fleet, on its way down the river, we will attempt to describe as graphically as possible the encounter of the *Galissoniere* with the forts at Kimpai, on the afternoon of Sunday, while the gunboats *Volta*, *Vipère*, *Aspic*, and *Lynx* were bombarding the forts and arsenal above Ma-moi.

One of the largest French ironclads on the China station, the *Galissoniere*, had for some days previous to the event I am about to relate, been anchored a short distance from the outer bar. Divine service was held under the shade of the awnings on the spar deck, when midst all the terrific engines and munitions of war, the hardy sailors bowed their uncovered heads, while the chaplain, in reverential voice offered thanks to Him, the Lord of Battles, for the victory achieved by their comrades the day before, and implored His blessing on the ship and crew so soon to be engaged in combat with the enemy. Shortly after, the mighty ship was seen to be underway and gradually approaching the entrance to the Kimpai Pass.

Inside the forts, the gunners were ready, standing match in hand, determined to give this bold intruder a warm reception. On, slowly, carefully on, came the great ship. Three hundred pair of eyes from her bridge and decks were keenly scrutinising the hillsides, and eagerly watching for the slightest sign of attack from the enemy. When within about two miles and a half from Kimpai, the full broadside of the huge vessel, all bristling with guns ready loaded and run out, was presented in defiance to the hidden fort.

Five minutes of suspense, then from the forts a tongue of flame shot out, followed by a puff of smoke and loud report. The projectile went wide of the mark. This was followed by two more, with the same result. Several more were fired in rapid succession, and then as if exasperated and entirely out of patience, the sides of the huge monster belched forth flame and smoke, and a shower of shell rained down upon the fortifications. The duel went on in this way some time, the shot from the forts falling all around the ship, and those from the ship encircling the forts with fiery hail. At length, a well directed ball from shore struck the *Galissonere*, followed by another, which also did execution. Apparently satisfied with this, the assailant turned about and steamed back to her anchorage off Sharp Peak, having engaged the forts nearly an hour. The intention of the captain of the *Galissonière* was to run as close in as possible, for the purpose of ascertaining the depth of the

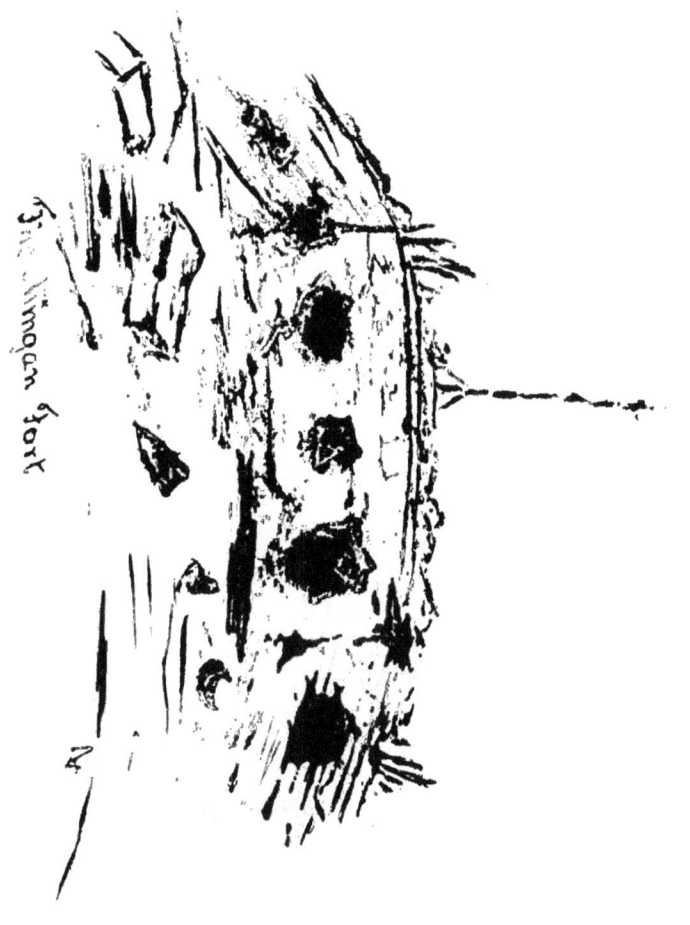

Dunamoan Fort

water, and if the passage had been interfered with in any way; and also to make himself thoroughly acquainted with the strength and calibre of the enemy's guns; the precision of their fire; and to form a rough estimate of the probable resistance to be encountered when it should please him to force his ship past the Kimpai forts.

The apparent retreat of one of the strongest vessels of the enemy from before the guns of the Chinese elated the defenders of the forts to such a degree that on the following day when the Captain of the s.s. *Namoa* went on shore to enquire why his vessel had been denied a passage, the commander of the forces told him that torpedoes were laid in the river, and that he was in hopes of giving a very warm reception to the French, when they should try to force the pass. The *Namoa* presently left for Amoy.

On Tuesday morning the French opened a furious bombardment on the Mingan forts. After heavy firing on the part of the assailants, with but feeble response from the defenders, the fortifications were all captured, guns spiked and burst with gun cotton, the earthworks levelled, and the hosts of His Imperial Majesty put to a precipitate flight, within the short space of three hours. It is reported that the Chinese warriors assembled on Kimpai heights, upon seeing the forts so quickly crumbling away before the terrific fire from the enemy's guns, took to flight instantly, and have not been seen in the neighbourhood since. The following morning, from the lofty peaks of the hills bordering the river Min, the French squadron were seen coming slowly down the stream, and to form themselves in battle array. When off the village of Quantao, situated a little above the Kimpai pass, out from the fleet came the great *Duguay Trouin*, slowly and cautiously feeling her way towards the entrance to the passage. The even watchful *de Paquax* discovered a small object just above the Kimpai point that excited his suspicions. Fire was opened upon this ill-fortified store-house of Chinese munitions of war. The few soldiers left to protect it, made but a faint show of resistance, and the guns were soon silenced.

As the tiny but trusty pilot fish goes before its huge master the shark, so did the small steam

launch carefully probe the way for its mighty
Leviathan. In the bow a man with a long pole
in his hand sounded the channel for torpedoes and
other hidden dangers, while the great *Duguay Trouin*
followed in the wake of her diminutive pilot. Chinese shot
and shell fell all about, but harmlessly, and the launch,
though exposed to a terrible fire, continued her dangerous
work. The Chang Mên, or White Fort, is on the left
geographical bank of the river, and near the entrance to
the Kimpai Pass. It commands the pass towards the
sea, and is more than two hundred feet above the sea
level. A safe passage having been found, this important
stronghold became the objective point for the guns of
the *Duguay Trouin*. The battery of this fort, like
those lately destroyed on the Mingan heights, was set in
solid masonry and trained in such a manner as to command the lower reaches of the river only; consequently
any attack made from above could not be repulsed with
fire from these guns. Entering the pass the *Duguay
Trouin* poured broadside after broadside into the sides
and rear of the Chang Mên, at the same time the men
in the tops rained down showers of Hotchkiss' balls
upon the luckless soldiers in and around the fortifications.
No opposition was encountered for some time, but at
length a band of the scattered braves collected on the hill
above the White Fort, and commenced to fire upon the
ship with rifles. The firing was thoroughly characteristic of the marksmen. In fairness it must be admitted
that a few stray bullets hit the water somewhere in the
vicinity of the object of attack; but by far the greater
number of shots buried themselves in the hills beyond,
and many travelled, and perhaps are still travelling,
towards the region of the moon. Of course being armed
with a loaded musket, and having received the command
to fire, in strict obedience it is necessary to discharge the
piece; but to aim at any particular object is superfluous,
and considered by the Chinese soldier as being outside
his instructions altogether. The Captain of the *Duguay
Trouin*, having satisfied himself both from the feeble fire
returned from the fortifications, and from the faint
attempts of the surrounding military to resist his
approach, that the forts were his whenever he chose to

Chinese Cannon "swett" by the French - Mission Inst

return and take them, turned his ship up stream and returned to the squadron. While the *Duguay Trouin* had been engaged as above related, another ship of the fleet was shelling a large fortified camp situated a little above the White Fort. Soon after the bombardment commenced fire broke out among the tents, spreading rapidly. Soon the whole encampment was in flames, the fire having found ready material in the baggage and inflammable huts of the soldiers.

At break of day on Thursday morning, the *Duguay Trouin* and *Triomphante* got up anchor, and steamed down the river to their stumping ground of the previous afternoon. A terrific fire was opened immediately upon the camps and fortifications on each side of the Kimpai Pass. Not the slightest resistance was made by any of these. The French guns continued to pour in a slow, steady fire upon the forts, without receiving a single gun in return. Towards noon, both ships, in farewell, threw such a shower of shot and shell against the sides of these forts that they literally crumbled away before the terrific storm. The vessels now proceeded down the river, shelling everything that looked like a camp or fortification on either hand. The defences below the Kimpai Pass were now to be bombarded. The first shell fell into one of these forts, the single occupant of which ran for his very life as the missile exploded. This statement will not convulse the world, as being the first recorded flight of a celestial from before the enemy's fire. Down from Mingan, now come the gunboats *Lynx* and *Volta*, runing close inshore, and finishing the work of their larger companions. As evening came on, the firing ceased, and when night closed upon Kimpai, it was unrecognizable as the apparently impregnable tower of strength of the previous evening.

The Chinese were reported to have sixty thousand warriors behind the heights of Kimpai. Where were they? All that could be seen during the day were a few very terrified military trying to hide themselves behind everything available, and as opportunity offered, to rapidly increase the distance between themselves and the enemy.

Friday morning opened with a desultory fire from the

Triomphante and *Duguay Trouin*, upon the already deserted and battered forts. The keen-eyed *Lynx* was there, ever and anon darting in and leaving a terrible landmark of solid iron. A deadly fire was kept up from her great guns and the Hotchkiss in the tops till nearly three o'clock in the afternoon, when the firing ceased from all the ships, and peace once more reigned over the waters of the Min. An hour and a half later five French ships left the river in the following order:—*Villars, Volta, D'Estaing, Chateau Renaud,* and *Lynx.* On the following day, in the afternoon, the *Duguay Trouin, La Galissoniere, Triomphante,* and *Vipère,* bound to Matsou, bade farewell to Kimpai waters.

Many persons, authorities on naval and military affairs, seem to have thought that the French would have great difficulty in passing the Mingan, Kimpai and White forts, but as I have shown, it was not so. These forts could not possibly offer resistance when attacked from the rear, for the obvious reason stated earlier in the chapter, that the defenders could not make use of the guns.

The loss on the side of the French was four men killed, one of these a Lieutenant, cousin of Capt. Encrad of the *Vipère,* to which vessel the deceased was attached at the time of his death. The unfortunate lady, the widow of this gallant young officer, is the sister of the great engineer Monsieur de Lesseps. May the sad bereavement fall lightly, and the knowledge that her husband meet a glorious death bravely defending his country's flag, make some slight atonement for the great loss.

We will now sail slowly down the river in our literary argos, and in passing review the damage done by the French forces. Starting from Spiteful Island we note that the large villages on the mainland opposite this island are still flourishing and the houses left unharmed by French shells.

The first fort on the left bank, slightly below these hamlets, did not fare so well, but has since been rebuilt; fresh earth and stones having been piled against its face. It is now apparently deserted. On the summit of a small hill sloping down to the water's edge, is a much

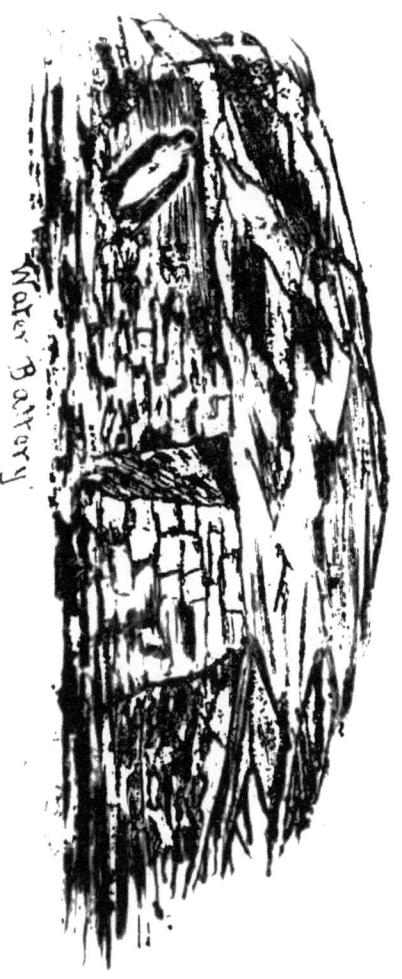
Water Battery

larger fortification than the last. Here many people were observed, some in a great state of bustle and activity, repairing the damage done by the shells. At the back of this, on a considerably higher eminence, may be seen the remains of an ancient fortified castle; but these ruins have been strangers for many centuries to the reports of guns within the walls.

We are now at the small fortified island. The defenses are in ruins, and apparently have been in a dilapidated condition for a number of years. Efforts were evidently made to mount guns upon the battlements. A cannon is lying at the base of the rock, near the water's edge, and several more are visible within the fort. The village on the mainland in the rear of this fort is very much battered, especially at the lower end, which is very close to a large water battery that is completely disabled, and the walls in some places levelled to the ground. The villages and forts on the left bank of the Mingan pass, all bear signs of having encountered the French shells. The villages were not bombarded purposely, and it is evident that their close proximity to the forts was the cause of the damage sustained on the right bank of the river. At the lower entrance to the pass is a very long water battery. Portions of this are razed to the ground, the houses inside the fortifications are battered down, and everything bears silent testimony to the fact that it was here that the French squadron did their heaviest firing. Three mounted guns can be seen within the fort, and gorgeous flags are waving again defiantly over the ruins; on the extreme point is a subterranean battery riddled by shell; the embrasures are enlarged to five times their original size. No signs of life and no guns are visible here. As we leave the pass the river widens considerably. Nothing worthy of attention is to be seen on either hand till in the distance we can distinguish the White Fort, and the entrance to the Kimpai Pass. Just before reaching the mouth of the pass can be seen a sunken wreck that drifted down from the engagement at Mamoi. There are also many junks partially submerged. These are intended, with the aid of more, to block the channel in case the enemy return. The Chang Mên is deserted. A solitary flagstaff marks its unadorned head. From the river nothing else is visible save the battered walls. In a small bay at the foot of the hill nestles a hamlet. Nine war junks, carrying each five diminutive cannon, are anchored off this place, having brought down soldiers a few days previously to reinforce the forts above. Many of the military were seen down around this village, but none near their quarters. On the opposite hillside of the river is a large forts with red stone wall running down the face of the hill to the water, culminating in a series of smaller defences. These are very much shattered and the guns in the upper part all burst. Two antique canonades, blown off short at the trunnions, are still standing on their carriages, defiant but unoffensive near the water front. The residences (or they might be called walled citadels) of the mandarins, are striking objects on the hillsides, and attract attention both by their imposing appearance, and the number of banners that adorn the walls. These mansions all seem to have escaped the shells of the French.

As we leave the Kimpai Pass on our left hand we see the ruins of several white-coloured forts on the hill slopes, and at the very summit of one a large sandstone fort apparently not damaged, with flagstaff in centre of the wall, and on each side of it two guns, one mounted on its carriage, the other lying on the masonry. No sign of life was to be seen anywhere near this fortification. Still on the left, a small island standing well out in the bay, has on its not very lofty summit a large yellow sandstone fort, some portions of it knocked away and others more or less damaged. Flags were flying in abundance and natives were seen passing in and out. On the right a strong fortification similar in construction crowns the highest point of a lofty hill. This stronghold was but slightly damaged, and from all external appearances has escaped the fate of so many of its companions, that only a short while ago looked down frowning and terrible from their commanding positions, upon the quiet waters of the now rapidly widening river Min. In two lines more we can tell about the sunken side-wheel steamer and the junks that are under water, their masts only being in sight. If we pass these the strong current

Interior of one of Kumbai Forts.

sweeping out of the broad estuary, will sweep us out to sea. Nothing can be more terrible than this, to be at sea in a literary sense.

It is evident that the French have disabled every one of these forts. From behind the ruins of several still peer forth the muzzles of field pieces placed in position since the departure of the enemy; but it will take a very long time, and a great number of men must be employed, and new material be expended, to restore these fortifications to anything like the former condition, or to make them in any way reliable strongholds. As we pass on towards the sea the only thing of interest to be seen is the French fleet anchored under the friendy shadow of Matsou.

Chapter VI.

RETROSPECT, COMPARISONS, AND OPINIONS.

We will now glance back at the memorable events that occurred in Foochow and its vicinity, between the twenty-third and thirtieth of August. A telegram arrived from Paris instructing Admiral Courbet to bombard the Arsenal at Foochow at sunrise of the twenty-second; to land French troops and destroy the war material and stores. As we have seen this was postponed owing to the inclemency of the weather, till noon of the twenty-third, when at fifty-five minutes after one the shelling of the forts and vessels at Pagoda Anchorage commenced. In twelve minutes the fighting on the water may be said to have ceased.

The resistance of the forts and arsenal above Mamoi, prolonged the bombardment for some three hours.

An exciting night was passed in witnessing conflagrations and warding off fire ships. The Sunday morning brought more firing and bloodshed, and the evening closed on a day of carnage.

Monday, the twenty-fourth, the French bade farewell to the Pagoda, and commenced operations above Mingan. At Mamoi, the residence of the English Consul was plundered. At the mouth of the river the mighty *Galis-*

soniere tested the strength of the Kimpai forts. Tuesday began the bombardment of Mingan in terrific earnest. All quiet at Kimpai. Up towards Foochow, the lowest class of natives recreated themselves by sending various obnoxious members of a social grade to that bourne, whence, even Mandarins, do not return. The argument was thus,—" Spose mandarins no have got, Flenchman no come makee bobbly." This proved conclusive enough to the victims.

Wednesday, the twenty-seventh, a day of victory. The White Fort and Kimpai fell. The English Admiral and American Captain while surveying the ruins of the fight at Mamoi, in their respective steam launches, were fired upon by persons pillaging on the Pagoda Island.

Thursday, the twenty-eighth, was aroused from its slumbers by the heavy guns of the *Duguay Trouin*, and *Triomphante* completing the destruction of the Kimpai Forts. The captain of the *Enterprise* and a resident citizen were again threatened by warlike demonstrations from armed natives on the crest of Pagoda hill.

Friday, twenty-ninth, slow firing on the camps at Kimpai. Departure of *Villars, Volta, D'Estaing, Chateau Renaud* and *Lynx* At Mamoi all quiet. At Foochow a crowd threatened the British Consul while he was standing reading various proclamations, promulgating the curious desire of the authorities to possess at any price the head pieces of their French enemies, and even those of their own poor defeated braves. Flight of the intimidated to the Viceroy's Yamen. Rapid change of garb; donning of queue; exit in sedan chairs, disguised and guarded. Fortunate escape, thanks to native cunning and Chinese blindness.

Saturday, thirtieth, all hail! joyful day to the people of Fo-kien. The dreaded enemy has left their shores, to return in anger not yet awhile, perhaps never. In peace and goodwill, it is to be hoped that the French tricolor will soon be borne up the River Min, to the heart of tea-scented Fo-kien.

At Pagoda Anchorage and Foochow, all is quiet, and trade gradually resuming its former busy proportions.

FRENCH FLEET ENGAGED AT MA-MOI.

No.	Name.	Class, &c.	Tonnage Disp.	Horse Power	No. of Crew.	Battery.			Damage Sustained, &c.
I.	Triomphante	2nd class casemated corvette, 6" armor plated.	4,127	2,400	410	6 Breech-loading Rifles,	9¾ cal.		None visible.
						1	,,	7¾ ,,	
						6	,,	5¼ ,,	
II.	Duguay Trouin	2nd class cruiser, composite.	3,189	3,740	300	5	,,	7¾ ,,	Hammock nettings amidships, starboard side, carried away by a shell.
						5	,,	5½ ,,	
III.	Villars	2nd class cruiser, wooden hull.	2,268	2,790	250	15	,,	5½ ,,	Struck a little forward of third after gun portside.
IV.	D'Estaing	,,	2,236	2,790	250	15	,,	5½ ,,	None visible.
V.	Volta	2nd class sloop, wooden hull.	1,300	1,000	160	3	,,	5½ ,,	Shot hole a little above the water line amidships, starboard side.
						3	,,	4 ,,	
VI.	Lynx	1st class gunboat.	452	...	120	3	,,	5½ ,,	None visible.
						2	,,	4 ,,	
VII.	Aspic	gunboat.	471	...	120	2	,,	5½ ,,	,, ,,
						2	,,	4 ,,	
VIII.	Vipère	,,	471	...	120	2	,,	5½ ,,	,, ,,
						2	,,	4 ,,	

CHINESE FLEET ENGAGED AT MA-MOI.

No.	Name.	Class, &c.	Tonnage Disp.	Horse Power.	No. of Crew.	Battery.	Damage Sustained, &c.
I.	Yang-woo	2nd class cruiser, composite hull.	1,400	250	270	Six Broadside 8½ tons Muzzle Loading Whitworths. Two 8½ tons " " Bow and Stern. One Pivot 6 tons " " abaft foremast.	Blown up by topedo boat—burnt—sunk and blew up.
II.	Foo-poo	3rd class sloop.	...	150	70	6 Broadside 45 pdr. Vavaseur B. L. R. 1 Pivot 10-inch Muzzle-loading Smooth Bore	Ran away up river, and saved herself. One shot through her. Sunk and back broken.
III.	Chi-an	"	...	150	150	6 Broadside 45 pdr. Vavaseur B. L. R. 1 Pivot, 4 tons Armstrong.	Burnt and sunk.
IV.	Fei-yuen	"	...	150	150	6 Broadside 45 pdr. Vavaseur B. L. R.	Burnt and sunk.
V.	Ching-vei	"	...	80	100	4 Broadside 45 pdr. Vavaseur B. L. R. 1 Pivot, 8½ ton Armstrong.	Sunk.
VI.	Fuh-sing	"	...	80	90	2 Broadside 45 pdr. Vavaseur B. L. R. 2 " 4" M. L. R. 1 Pivot, 8½ ton M. L. Whitworths.	Sunk.
VII.	Yu-sing	Sloop.	...	...	30	8 small brass guns, built by cadet engineers as ex-criminent.	Sunk.
VIII.	Yang-pao		...	150	150	Hull copied from Yang-woo. No guns.	Yang pao, sunk off Arsenal.
IX.	Chun-hing	Transports.				Intended for ramming purposes.	Chun-hing, burnt and sunk.
X.	Chin-shing	Mosquito boats, built after A.B. class, iron hulls.	...	389	30	One 16-ton gun.	Both sunk.
XI.	Fuh-shing						

A glance at the foregoing tables is sufficient to show the great superiority of the French fleet over that of their enemies, though not in the actual number of vessels. It is nevertheless at once apparant that the great advantage in tonnage and armament of the French ships, more than compensated for the great disparity in numerical strength. The Chinese had a larger number of vessels by three times than their antagonists; but of what class were these so-called war ships? We will now compare with each other the largest vessels on both sides that were engaged in the action of the 23rd of August.

The *Triomphante*, the vessel of greatest tonnage on the side of the French, is a second rate sea-going ironclad of 4,127 tons, ship-rigged, compound engines of 2,400 indicated horse power, full sail power and a maximum speed of thirteen knots, having an armored belt and casemate varying from six inches in its greatest to four inches in its least thickness, over a wooden backing of twenty-six inches. The iron belt encircles the water line to the height of the main deck beams, the casemate carrying the armour to the spar deck from some distance forward of the smoke-stack to a few feet abaft the mainmast, thus protecting the most vulnerable part of the ship, the engines and boilers. Two barbette turrets are over the forward corners of the casemate, and contain each a 5½ inch breech-loading rifle, under the forecastle 7¼ inch breech-loading rifle, working in a single port. Six 9¼ inch breech-loading rifles act as broadside guns on the main deck. An extra strong bow, armed with a bronze ram, completes the armament of this formidable vessel. The *Galissoniere* and *Bayard* are of this class.

The *Yang-woo* was the largest and considered by native naval authorities to be the most reliable vessel in the Foochow division. A second class cruiser of 1,400 tons displacement, composite hull, non-compound engines of 250 indicated horse power, ship-rigged, full sailing power, and an average speed of eight knots. A battery of six muzzle-loading Whitworth guns 3½ tons each, acted as broadside on the spar deck; two of the same weight and calibre on the forecastle as bow-chasers, and another of the same dimensions and character occupying a similar position astern. One Whitworth pivot gun of six tons, abaft the foremast, completes the armament of this vessel.

The vessel next in size to the *Triomphante* is the *Duguay Trouin*, of 3,198 tons displacement, ship-rigged with compound engines of 3,740 indicated H.P., full sail power and a maximum speed of 16 knots. This corvette has an iron hull sheathed with wood and copper, a strengthened bow for ramming, armed with a heavy bronze ram. Four half turrets or platforms on each side of the spar deck, projecting out from the side of the ship so as to give a clear fore and aft fire. The turrets each contain a breech loading rifle of $7\frac{3}{4}$ inches calibre, and a bow-chaser of the same character works under the forecastle in a single port. A B.L.R. $5\frac{1}{2}$ inches calibre, mounted in barbette on a centre-pivot carriage, performs the same duties astern. Four rifles of this class are placed as broadsides on the spar deck. The battery is carried on the spar deck, thus leaving a clear roomy main deck.

It is difficult to decide on the next in order to the *Yang-woo*, in the Chinese fleet. The three, *Foo-poo*, *Chi-an* and *Fei-yuen*, gunboat sloops all of similar size and armament, must be placed after the flagship for want of an intermediate grade.

Wooden hulls, brig and brigantine rigged, and non-compound engines of 150 H.P. The first carrying a battery of six breech-loading forty-five pounders, (Vavaseur's) and one muzzle-loading Armstrong pivot of about ten inches calibre. The second the same broadside and a 4 ton Armstrong pivot. The third (the *Fei-yuen*) six Vavaseur broadside guns, but no pivot.

This comparison carried to a greater length would become invidious, when such ships as the *Villars* and *D'Estaing* are placed side by side with the *Ching-Wai* and *Fuh-shing*, fourth rate gunboat sloops.

The vast superiority of a ship like the *Triomphante* over the *Yang-woo* is so evident, that even were both vessels manned with crews of equal strength, intrepidity, and discipline, a duel between the two, no matter how much circumstances favored the smaller one, could not last more than a few minutes, or perhaps seconds. At close quarters within a confined area, the guns of the *Yang-woo* could not be loaded again after the first broadside had been fired. Riflemen in the enemy's tops, and sharpshooters from the decks, stationed for the purpose could pick off the spongers and loaders as fast as they made their appearance, and a great many of the gun's crew that would have to expose themselves inboard. The men on the decks of the French ship need not be exposed to a like treatment from the enemy, owing to the shelter obtained in the barbettes and underneath the forecastle.

The spar deck broadside battery is uncovered, but the guns are breech loaders and the bulwarks ball proof.

To draw comparison, however light, between a vessel like the *Duguay Trouin* and the *Foo-Poo* would be absurd.

Setting aside the fact that the French had machine guns and that their antagonists had not, and supposing that the vessels on both sides had had crews of equal valor and numerical strength, and been well officered, it is improbable, nay almost impossible, that the result could have been anything but a disastrous defeat to the squadron of smaller vessels, though outnumbering the enemy by three to one.

Giving the French the advantage of machine guns and a superior torpedo service, the issue of the contest became a certainty, and it only remained to be seen what revelations would be made in the science of modern warfare. In this engagement, the potency of machine guns and their incalculable value in naval combat, and the efficacy of a well trained and thoroughly capable torpedo service, was made manifest to the world. The continued hail of shell from Hotchkiss cannon in the tops of the French men-of-war upon their antagonists, swept them down like wheat before the mower. Relays of men could not be brought up from below fast enough to fill up the gaps in the gun's crews. The diminutive shell came crashing through the sides and bulwarks of the ship. Splinters flying in every direction killed many more. So destructive were the torrents of iron poured upon these vessels, that it is estimated eight hundred of the thousand computed to have been on the Chinese ships were killed. Vast numbers of men—every French ship having more than one half its complement in excess—were able to work both broadsides at once and batter everything to pieces on each hand with their heavy guns, and at the same time rain down showers of bullets from their light artillery in the tops, which were completely destructive to all life on the decks of the Chinese vessel. They had nothing to resist the like of this. Their ships were but half manned, and with *ci-devant* crews of soldiers and rice coolies at that. The men could not be brought to be work the batteries in the face of the destructive hail from the French machine guns, and, to crown all, the majority of officers were absent from their posts, and those who were at their stations, with a few notable exceptions, exemplified the aphorism that discretion is the better part of valor. The damage done by the machine guns to the government property at the Arsenal, is almost incredible. The walls are literally riddled. The Chinese had Gatling guns on hand in the Arsenal, and application had been made for them by the Captains of the *Yang-Woo* and other vessels, but the request was refused by the higher naval officials.

The machine gun used principally by the French in the late engagement was Hotchkiss Revolving Cannon, an American invention "introduced into naval services with the especial objects of, first, repelling torpedo and boarding attacks ; second, for use against light merchant vessels, where a light, long artillery fire is most effective. The gun has five barrels and can be fired at a rate of from sixty to eighty shots a minute ; its ammunition is shell and case-shot, the weight of projectiles ranging from one and a half pounds in the light calibre, to six pounds in the heavy one." The only rival of this gun at present is the Nordenfeft, which is extensively used in some navies in preference to the Hotchkiss.

Before closing this essay we will glance at the two gunboats, *Chin-shing* and *Fuh-sing* of the Chinese squadron, as being really for their size the most reliable vessels engaged at Foochow. Iron twin-screw gunboats of 440 tons displacement, of 389 indicated horse power, and a maximum speed of ten through a musket proof bow port. An hydraulic loading apparatus underneath the covered forecastle, magazines and shell rooms under the gun with side hatches and railway for transporting ammunition to the muzzle. These gunboats had they been properly manned and well officered could have caused much trouble to the enemy, at a comparatively safe distance to themselves. At a long range they would have a far better chance of hitting than of being hit. China has many of this class of river boats, and two, English built attached to the northern division, that rank second to none of their kind. The shore defences at Mamoi were wretched in the extreme. The water batteries at the foot of the Pagoda hill were considered by the natives as almost impregnable. Six antique cannonades, eight small cannon, firing a ball averaging from eight to ten pounds, and three antediluvian field pieces, completed the armaments of these loosely piled up fortifications. The Mingan and Kimpai forts were defended with Armstrong and Krupp guns.

A short sketch of the constitution of the naval and military service of H.I.M. the Emperor of China, will close this chapter.

The Chinese army and navy have degenerated sadly since the early days of the present dynasty, when the Manchoo Emperors had to maintain their power by arms. These were palmy days for the garrisons stationed throughout the kingdom and kept in an effective state. Guns were cast and placed in battery and on the walls of the large cities, and the troops were well supplied with arms and all necessaries. Strict obedience to the laws, civil and military, was enforced, and swift was the punishment inflicted on the head of the political agitator. But as centuries rolled on, decay crept in. The dynasty found itself seated firmly on the Imperial throne, with the laws of government well in hand. Internal troubles were no longer to be apprehended, and China was at peace with the outside world.

The secret of thorough military organization and effective administration has been lost, and at present there do not exist in the world more wretched troops, worse equipped, more undisciplined, more insensible to honor, or in a word more aburd.

The principal causes of inefficiency are as follows. First, a protracted peace of some centuries ; second, the Manchoo policy, which seeks to perpetuate an unwarlike spirit and general feebleness on the natives, that still prevent them from ever attempting to shake off the Tartar yoke ; third, the undiscerning pertinacity of the government, which has until recently refused to sanction any reform in the tactics and weapons of ancient times ; and lastly the great importance attached to literary pursuits, which permeates the whole political system, and the consequent reproach thrown upon the profession of arms, which is entered solely by physical qualifications.

Both the army and navy are recruited from among the inferior classes of society, and the fact that officers and men are alike liable to corporal punishment may in some measure account for the very low *morale* which they possess.

Yet the Chinese are not without bravery. In the last affair at Canton, the troops distinguished themselves in fighting against the English, and also up the Peiho in 1859, and it is highly probable that if they were properly drilled, disciplined, and officered, and supplied with the munitions of war, they would make soldiers superior to most Asiatics.

Very little distinction is made between the regulations for the naval and military forces which both come under the Ping-Poo, or Board of War, the central administration at Pekin. The general administration is divided amongst coast districts, at each of which is a dockyard for construction and repair. These districts have each a distinct corresponding fleet division. First, Canton squadron, second Foochow squadron, third Nanking squadron, and fourth the squadron of Li Hung-chang in the north. At Foochow are the principal machine shops and building yard ; Shanghai, Nanking and Tientsin has a powder factory and Arsenal ; and at Canton there are the naval school ships. For centuries China made but little advance in naval affairs. The long period of isolation to which the country subjected itself, the vast inland territory acknowledging the sway of the Emperor, and the fact that the Chinese people are entirely unsuited to naval enterprise, will in some manner account for the state of the service.

The progress made within the last forty years is remarkable for China; but still propositions for the further improvement of this important branch of the protective service, do not meet with that ready acceptance and advancement at Pekin, which foreigners are led to expect from a country professedly anxious to shake off the lethargy of centuries and take its place in the foremost rank of nations.

"Each province in China is antonomous, or nearly so, and the supreme authorities, whether Viceroys or Governors, are practically independent so long as they act in accordance with the very minute details laid down for their guidance. The principal functions of the Pekin Government are to see that these regulations are carried out, and in case they should not be, to call the offending Viceroy or Governor to account. Each Viceroy raises his own army, and navy, which he pays, or unfortunately sometimes does not pay, out of the revenues of his government. He levies his own taxes, and except in particular cases, is the final court of appeal in all judicial matters within the limits of his rule. Official purity and justice must be treated as comparative terms in China."

The long period of official oppression that the Chinese have undergone, has made them essentially an unwarlike people; not peace-living but fright-fearing; and the act of tyranny must be severe indeed, to arouse them from their torpor. The manner of conscription on the very lowest class, the indefinite term of service; the practice of transferring men from the army to the navy, and *vice versa*; the purchase system; the unscrupulous conduct and general incapacity of the officers; and the extreme indifference manifested at Pekin, all combine to make the army and navy of H.I.M. a very doubtful protective force. With affairs in this state can the government be surprised at the feeble resistance offered and the total destruction of a naval division and arsenal?

China has few sympathizers in her present difficulty. In the hour of prosperity, instead of opening up her resources and welcoming other nations to her ports, an overbearing pride and haughty isolation have been her chief characteristics.

Should the present trouble be decided by force of arms alone, it is at once obvious that France would be victorious. But should Chinese cunning and artifice get the upper hand, and gain a victory over French diplomacy, the position of all foreigners would be unbearable. "China cannot be trusted with victory." Until the government adopts a more liberal policy both at home and abroad, and shows signs of progressing, the arrogance of China must be held in check by the forces single or combined of European powers. But China must first look to herself. The government has far more to fear from its own subjects, than from the enemy at present destroying its navies, bombarding its Arsenals, and demolishing its property.

Events are daily showing us that the Chinese people are ready *for revolt*; to. rise against their hated oppressors and petty tyrants—the mandarins, and strive to shake off the yoke that has for centuries been grinding them down, till at last they dare no longer call their lives their own.

The doctrine inculcated from time immemorial by the highest constitutional authorities, and the learned Confucius among others, has been almost forgotten, that the duties existing between the Emperor and his people are reciprocal and that so long as the rule of the sovereign is just and beneficent, it is the duty of the people to render strict and willing obedience; but should he depart from the paths of rectitude and virtue, it is equally incumbent on their part to resist his authority to the utmost. The Chinese people cannot see as far as this. They can only *feel* the hand of the *nearer* oppressor.

It is a difficult matter to estimate the power of the Emperor. "The outside world sees only the Imperial bolts, but how they are forged, or whose is the hand that shoots them no one can tell." The throne is so hedged with ceremonies that unless the occupant be a man of supreme ability he cannot fail to fall under the guidance of his ministers and favorites. What the

Chinese people want, what they must do, before they can find a potent means of protection against the oppression of the subordinate officials of the government, is to break down the barriers around the throne! The French have unknowingly given the initiative, and the natives in some districts have already seized upon it.

China is like a large pie. For many years covetous nations have been nibbling at the edge of the crust. Now a crack is made a new and strange agency is at work more towards the centre, beyond the extreme border. This will gradually spread over the rich-rounded surface of the interior in a series of convulsions till it finds the apex, the summit, where all the leaf-like ornamentations are, and hidden away in these, almost covered, will be found a young boy! The sudden influx of light will cause to crumble away all the ancient surroundings, and over the ruins and ceremonies of centuries will step out before the world, free and untrammelled H.I.M. the Emperor of the Flowery Land!

Do not suppose for an instant that we anticipate in China a revolution like that in France—total overthrow and destruction of the monarchy. Not this, but merely that a trembling of the pie crust, brought about by coolie wrongs, will cause the downfall of many ancient structures and monuments of antiquity; and that in the crack occasioned by this pie-quake, mandarin oppression and bigotry, despotism and coolie slavery, may find a grave, and European and American enterprise a virgin soil, in which the roots of trade may take such firm hold that convulsions, however great, may never again retard the growth of the flourishing tree.

THE NAVAL & MILITARY PRESS
Specialist Books For The Serious Student Of Conflict

Military book enthusiasts now have a place on the internet dedicated to themselves. Our site is the most extensive devoted to military history on the web. You can browse and shop through our vast range of titles by time period or by theme, or use our advanced search facilities to find areas of specific interest.

The Naval & Military Press Ltd was founded in 1991 and quickly established itself as a mecca for the military enthusiast. Over 35,000 customers worldwide enjoy receiving our booklist which contains many hundreds of first-class books. With the advances in technology we are now pleased to show all of you with access to the internet our full catalogue. Updated regularly, you can count on the same level of service that our existing customers enjoy.

Our own publications feature strongly on both our list and our website. The innovative approach we have to military bookselling and our commitment to publishing have made us Britain's leading independent military bookseller.

Many titles featured on this website are not unavailable through any other source in the world.

www.naval-military-press.com

General Sir Ian Hamilton's
Staff Officer's Scrap-Book during the Russo–Japanese War 1904–1905
9781474538077

As Hamilton was the military attaché of the British Indian Army serving with the Japanese army in Manchuria during the Russo-Japanese War, he was well placed to publish in 1907 this impressive eye witness account to a military confrontation between a well-known European army and a less-familiar Asian army. Good maps (many in colour), a full index and 600+ pages make this facsimile two-volume set a fine reference for the modern scholar, of a war that is still the classic example of a conflict waged for purely imperialistic motives, a rivalry for the control of Korea and Manchuria and indeed for the mastery of the Far East and China.

The Golden Chersonese and the way thither
9781905748198

A delightful description of her travels in Malaya and China in the 1880s by that intrepid lady Isabella L. Bird, first female member of the Royal Geographical Society and doyenne of all women travel writers.

NOTES FROM A JOURNAL OF RESEARCH INTO THE NATURAL HISTORY OF THE COUNTRIES VISITED DURING THE VOYAGE OF H.M.S. SAMARANG under the command of Captain Sir Edward Belcher, C.B., F.R.A.S.
9781905748013

Like Darwin on the Beagle, surgeon Arthur Adams was a naturalist with this 1843-45 Naval expedition to Japan and the Indian and China Seas. Contains fascinating descriptions of the region's flora and fauna.

LOW`S HISTORY of the INDIAN NAVY
9781474536530

This is an extremely rare work, in its original edition, and covers the life span of the Indian Navy, 1600 to 1863. Operations from the Persian Gulf to the Burma and First China Wars, from Aden to New Zealand and the Maori Wars, and the Indian Mutiny. Survey work from the Red Sea to the China Seas.

NARRATIVE OF THE EARL OF ELGIN'S MISSION TO CHINA AND JAPAN IN THE YEARS 1857, '58, '59
9781905748051

Superbly illustrated two-volume account of Lord Elgin's expeditions to the Far East in 1857-59 which resulted in the occupation of Canton, the burning of Peking's Imperial Summer Palace; and the opening of Japan to European trade.

"CHINA JIM" Being Incidents and Adventures in the Life of an Indian Mutiny Veteran
9781845748463

An account of the author's experiences in the Indian Mutiny and the Second China War. The author acquired his nickname as a result of the immense amount of loot he acquired from the Summer Palace at Peking!

CHINESE WAR, AN ACCOUNT OF ALL THE OPERATIONS OF THE BRITISH FORCES 1842
9781843428176
Detailed account of the first Chinese 'Opium war' with Britain. With 53 fascinating illustrations.

VOYAGE OF HIS MAJESTY'S SHIP ALCESTE, to China, Corea, and the Island of Lewchew, with an account of her shipwreck
9781905748068
Rather aptly summed up by the title, this book was written by the ship's surgeon on the 'Alceste' which was charged with delivering the British Embassy of Lord Amherst to China in 1816. Passing through Rio de Janeiro, the Cape of Good Hope and Batavia en-route, they arrived in the China Sea in the summer and their first meetings with the Chinese together with some of the politics of the time are described here.

OFFICIAL ACCOUNT OF THE MILITARY OPERATIONS IN CHINA 1900-1901
9781783311156
This official account of the military operations in China at the time of the Boxer Rebellion and the siege of the Foreign Legations in Peking was originally compiled by Major Norrie, a member of the Intelligence Staff of the British Contingent, China Field Force. It was considerably revised, edited and expanded by the Intelligence Department at the War Office. It begins with the rise of the Boxer Secret Society and the outbreak of hostilities against foreigners in the northern provinces, extends to cover the operations for the relief of Foreign Legations in Peking and concludes with the peace negotiations and withdrawal of the greater part of the allied forces from China, original editions are excessively rare.

THE CRUISE OF THE PEARL WITH AN ACCOUNT OF THE OPERATIONS OF THE NAVAL BRIGADE IN INDIA
9781843428206
Drawn from the unusual diary of a naval Chaplain detailing the exploits of a scratch Naval Brigade, consisting of warship crews fighting on shore, in quelling the Indian Mutiny in 1857-58. Charming, despite the grim nature of much of the material.

THE LAST CRUISE OF THE "MAJESTIC"
George Goodchild from the log book of Petty Officer J.G. Cowie
9781474539166

Interesting personal account of the service of battleship "Majestic" in the Dardanelles arranged by Goodchild from the logbook of Petty Officer J.G. Cowie. "Majestic" was a Majestic-class pre-dreadnought battleship. In early 1915, she was dispatched to the Mediterranean for service in the Dardanelles Campaign. She participated in bombardments of Turkish forts and supported the Allied landings at Gallipoli. On 27 May 1915, she was torpedoed by the German submarine U-21 at Cape Helles, sinking with the loss of 49 men.

THE COMMISSION OF HMS TERRIBLE 1898-1902
9781843425533

Naval Brigades in South African War & China 1900. Various nominal rolls.

THE NAVAL BRIGADE IN SOUTH AFRICA DURING THE YEARS 1877-78-79
9781843429203

An account of the actions of the Naval Brigade from 'HMS Active' in South Africa's Kaffir and Zulu wars in 1877-79. Written by the Brigade's principal medical officer.

THE HISTORY OF THE BALTIC CAMPAIGN OF 1854, FROM DOCUMENTS AND OTHER MATERIALS FURNISHED BY VICE-ADMIRAL SIR C. NAPIER
9781845742126

A full history of the Crimean War's 'forgotten' sideshow in the Baltic, based on the papers of the British Commander, Admiral Napier, which exonerates him from charges of incompetence.

www.ingramcontent.com/pod-product-compliance
Lightning Source LLC
Chambersburg PA
CBHW071316110426
42743CB00042B/2642